AS Psychology

Revision Guide for OCR

Claire Barker

Published by Inducit Learning Ltd trading as pushmepress.com,

Pawlett House, West Street, Somerton,

Somerset TA11 7PS, United Kingdom

www.pushmepress.com

First published in 2013

ISBN: 978-1-909618-18-3

All rights reserved. No part of this publication may be reproduced, stored in a retrieval system, or in any form or by any means, without the prior permission in writing of the publisher, nor otherwise circulated in any form of binding or cover other than that in which it is published and without a similar condition including this condition bring imposed on the subsequent publisher.

© Inducit Learning Ltd

Cartoons used with permission © Becky Dyer

All images © their respective owners

Contents

Preface 5
G541 – RESEARCH METHODS   5
G542 – CORE STUDIES AND APPROACHES   6

Research Methods 7
EXPERIMENTAL RESEARCH METHODS   7
NON-EXPERIMENTAL RESEARCH METHODS   11
EXAM RESCUE REMEDY   19

The Social Approach to Psychology 21
MILGRAM - OBEDIENCE TO AUTHORITY   22
PILIAVIN, RODIN AND PILIAVIN - THE SUBWAY SAMARITAN   27
REICHER AND HASLAM - THE BBC PRISON STUDY   32

The Physiological Approach to Psychology 37
SPERRY - 'SPLIT BRAIN' PATIENTS   38
DEMENT AND KLEITMAN - SLEEPING AND DREAMING   43
MAGUIRE - TAXI DRIVERS' BRAINS   48

The Cognitive Approach to Psychology 53
LOFTUS AND PALMER - EYEWITNESS TESTIMONY   54
BARON-COHEN ET AL - AUTISM IN ADULTS   58
SAVAGE-RUMBAUGH ET AL - LANGUAGE ACQUISITION IN CHIMPANZEES 63

Developmental Approach to Psychology 69
FREUD - LITTLE HANS   70
SAMUEL AND BRYANT - CONSERVATION   75
BANDURA, ROSS AND ROSS - IMITATION OF AGGRESSION   80

The Individual Differences Approach to Psychology 85
ROSENHAN - 'BEING SANE IN INSANE PLACES'   86
THIGPEN AND CLECKLEY - MULTIPLE PERSONALITY DISORDER (MPD)   91
GRIFFITHS - FRUIT MACHINE GAMBLING   95
Confusions to avoid   98

Perspectives in Psychology 99
PSYCHODYNAMIC PERSPECTIVE   99
BEHAVIOURIST PERSPECTIVE   100

Exam Rescue Remedy 101

Glossary of Key Terms 103

References 113
CORE STUDIES   113
GENERAL   115

Postscript 117

Preface

This revision aid is not designed as a comprehensive text book and you should follow any advice given by your teacher. As with any such book this is based solely on my interpretation of the original material, but if you are in any doubt you should refer to the original articles as this is what OCR examines.

I have given definitions of the main terms used in this book in the final section titled 'Glossary'. You will see these words used in bold throughout the text. In addition there are further words also in bold which are more specific to the particular chapters. You will find definitions for these under 'Key terms' at the end of each chapter. However, for brevity's sake, if a word has appeared in a previous chapter I have not repeated the definition.

G541 – RESEARCH METHODS

This first unit is worth 30% of your AS level and is described in the first chapter. It considers issues central to how research in psychology is carried out and the decisions that researchers have to take before, during and after completing a study. It covers various aspects of research methods, particularly the difference between experimental and non-experimental methods. Within these divisions it will further consider individual research methods, which for experimental methods includes laboratory experiments, field experiments and natural/quasi experiments. For non-experimental methods it looks at self-reports and observations and their various sub-divisions, and also correlations. There are some quite complicated terms used in this section and these are fully explained in the glossary at the end of the book. It is important that you as the student are familiar with these and can use them confidently and in context in your exam.

G542 – CORE STUDIES AND APPROACHES

This second unit is much longer and is worth 70% of your AS level in psychology. As it is so big there are many more chapters to help you with the finer points of this unit. You will find these chapters conveniently broken down by approach containing the three studies you have been taught. The specific detail about each approach can be found at the beginning of each chapter, whilst the synoptic links between the approach and the study are discussed at the end of each study. You will be able to refer to the glossary at the end of the book for some of the terminology used in this section; however, where some language is specific to a study this will be described in the 'Key terms' section at the end of the study to help you easily locate it. The first time a word or term that appears in either the glossary or key terms section appears in either the glossary or key terms section is used, it will be in bold capitals, but this may not be the case for subsequent uses, thus you will need to use your initiative at times and look through these sections.

Research Methods

Research Methods in psychology are broadly split between experimental methods and non-experimental methods. The choice of research method will depend very much on what you are trying to study and some are better suited to certain types of research than others and as such each have their own strengths and weaknesses.

EXPERIMENTAL RESEARCH METHODS

An experimental method will be selected when you wish to test a difference between two conditions and because of this is often referred to as 'a test of difference'.

Laboratory experiment

This is usually highly controlled and carried out in an unnatural environment. A lab experiment is considered by some to be the only true experimental method as participants can be randomly allocated to one condition or another.

Field experiment

This can offer some element of control as participants can be exposed to different conditions but it is carried out in a natural environment.

Natural/quasi experiment

Usually with a natural experiment the independent variables are naturally occurring and cannot be manipulated artificially e.g. gender, age. Because this limits the control that the experimenter has it is considered 'quasi', or not quite a true experiment.

Despite the differences between these types of experiments there are criteria that are common to all which need to be considered when carrying out experiments or answering questions about them.

Firstly it is important to remember that an experiment is a test of difference. If you think you are doing something else then it is not an experiment. All experiments should generate fully operationalised **ALTERNATE** and **NULL HYPOTHESES**. You should take steps to control **EXTRANEOUS VARIABLES** and ensure that they do not become **CONFOUNDING VARIABLES** and confuse the results.

You must select a representative sample from your target population to be able to generalise the results back to the target population. You will also need to make a decision on the most appropriate research design to use from **INDEPENDANT SAMPLES, REPEATED MEASURES** or **MATCHED PAIRS**.

Issues of standardisation and control need to be taken into account as this will ensure the **RELIABILITY** and **VALIDITY** of the experiment.

These need to be weighed up against issues of **ECOLOGICAL VALIDITY** and **MUNDANE REALISM**.

As with any psychological research ethical issues need to be considered to protect both the participants and the experimenter.

It is only with a test of difference that we can infer a cause and effect relationship and the robustness of this will depend on the **LEVEL OF DATA** obtained.

It is important to establish what level of data you have in order to select the appropriate **DESCRIPTIVE STATISTICS** and if relevant the correct **INFERENTIAL STATISTICAL TEST**.

Key terms

- **CAUSE AND EFFECT** - this is where the manipulated IV is the 'cause' and the measured DV is the 'effect'. Thus it cannot be inferred with correlations which simply have two variables.

- **CONTROL (experimental)** - this is anything which is kept the same within all conditions of an experiment.

- **INFERENTIAL STATISTICS (test)** - these are statistical techniques that measure the probability of a result being due to chance.

- **OPERATIONALISED** - this refers to the specific way you have chosen to measure or categorise your variables.

- **STANDARDISATION** - this refers to the process of making instructions or procedures consistent for all participants in an experiment.

- **TEST OF DIFFERENCE** - this describes the intention of an experiment.

Confusions to avoid

- A field experiment takes place in a natural environment and should not be confused with a natural experiment which refers to the independent variables.

- Students often describe an opportunity sample as one where you 'randomly select anyone who is available'. This colloquial use of the word 'random' means that they are then not able to adequately describe a random sample.

NON-EXPERIMENTAL RESEARCH METHODS

A non-experimental method would be considered when you wish to explore people's attitudes, opinions and feelings about a certain issue or when you wish to observe how people behave in a particular situation.

Self Reports

These are primarily used to explore attitudes, opinions and feelings. Students often mistake self-reports as only being about questionnaires but they can also include surveys and interviews.

Questionnaires

These can be either given out online or as a paper copy and consist of a set of questions that the participant will read and write the answers to. They may do it in front of the experimenter but more likely will be returned to the experimenter at a later time or date.

The questionnaire may use **OPEN QUESTIONS**, **CLOSED QUESTIONS**, **FIXED RESPONSE QUESTIONS** or **SCALED QUESTIONS** (such as **LIKERT SCALES**), or a mixture of all of these.

Surveys

These are essentially the same as a questionnaire but the experimenter asks the questions and fills in the responses that the participant gives.

Interviews

These are usually conducted face-to-face or maybe done over the telephone. They can take several formats; structured, semi-structured or unstructured.

- **STRUCTURED INTERVIEW** – all the questions are pre-defined and there is no deviation from these. This makes for easy analysis of the transcripts but can limit the amount of information that the experimenter can gather.

- **SEMI-STRUCTURED INTERVIEW** – this is much more flexible in its approach as it will have lead questions on specific topics but allows the experimenter to expand and deviate when interesting issues arise.

- **UNSTRUCTURED INTERVIEWS** – this permits the participant to discuss whatever they wish to about a topic. Although this makes it very open and flexible it also means it is extremely difficult to analyse the data.

As with experiments there are common criteria to be considered across the various self-report methods. We have mentioned the types of questions that could be selected but it should be remembered that **LEADING QUESTIONS** should be avoided to prevent compromising the integrity of the research.

Self-reports can only measure people's attitudes, opinions and feelings and it does not necessarily follow that their behaviour will mirror this. Often people will say they believe one thing and will then do something else.

Self-reports are particularly prone to **DEMAND CHARACTERISTICS** and **SOCIAL DESIRABILITY BIAS** both of which may be unintentional.

In addition, if the research is **SOCIALLY SENSITIVE** the participants may find the questions too embarrassing to answer honestly or they might even misunderstand the questions. This means that the **VALIDITY** and **RELIABILITY** will be reduced.

Finally, particularly with questionnaires, you need to take into account that response rates are typically very poor.

Key terms

- **CLOSED QUESTIONS** - these are questions that typically have a 'yes' or 'no' answer.

- **FIXED RESPONSE** - this is similar to a closed question but can include more responses such as 'other', 'sometimes' or 'don't know'.

- **LEADING QUESTIONS** - these are questions which direct a person to a specific answer or make it extremely unlikely that they would give a response that contradicts what the researcher wants.

- **LIKERT SCALE** - this is used as a measure of attitude in response to a statement. Typically there are five levels in the scale ranging from 'strongly agree' to 'strongly disagree'.

- **OPEN QUESTION** - this type of question does not have a predetermined response but allows the participant to give a free account of their opinions.

- **SOCIALLY SENSITIVE** - this defines research that may have implications or social consequences for the respondent. For example if you ask a person about the number of sexual partners they have had this may have an effect on their current relationship.

Confusions to avoid

- Reported attitudes are not necessarily the same as a person's behaviour. We often say one thing and do another.

- Questionnaires are **NOT** the only form of self-report and must not be confused as such in the exam.

Observations

These are usually used when the experimenter wishes to see how people actually behave in certain situations. Observations can be used independently of other research methods or as a tool to support them.

As with self-reports there are a variety of observational methods available to the experimenter.

- **CONTROLLED OBSERVATION** - the experimenter might manipulate variables in either an artificial or natural setting in order to observe whether people behave differently or the same. This is often used in conjunction with the field experiment method.

- **PARTICIPANT OBSERVATION** - the observer becomes part of the environment which they are observing and can be either **DISCLOSED** (overt) or **UNDISCLOSED** (covert).

- **NATURAL OBSERVATION** - this is a non-participant method of observation. The experimenter observes naturally occurring situations without affecting the environment in any way.

There are several important considerations for observational research that make it quite labour intensive.

Firstly you will need to consider **CODING SCHEMES** of the behaviour you wish to observe to ensure **INTER-RATER RELIABILITY**. In addition to this all the observers will need to be trained to facilitate this. And secondly an effective data collection sheet will need to be devised such as a tally chart.

You also need to decide how you will carry out your observation;

whether to use **TIME SAMPLING** or **EVENT SAMPLING**.

Finally the same considerations apply as to ethics, levels of data, descriptive statistics and if appropriate inferential statistics.

Key terms

- **CODING SCHEME** - this refers to a method typically used in observations which describes how a particular behaviour should be measured. For example 'aggression' might have a coding scheme that would include the number of times a child hits, slaps, kicks, punches, swears, shouts, threatens another child.

- **DISCLOSED** - this is where the participants of an observation are aware of the person who is carrying out the observation. It is sometimes referred to as an 'overt' observation.

- **EVENT SAMPLING** - this is where an event (or behaviour) is recorded every time it occurs.

- **TALLY CHART** - this is a simple method of recording the frequency of an event by ticking a box each time it occurs.

- **TIME SAMPLING** - this is where the behaviour of an individual is recorded at set time intervals, for example every 30 seconds.

- **UNDISCLOSED** - this is where the participants of an observation are unaware of the person observing them. It is sometimes referred to as a 'covert' observation.

Confusions to avoid

- Students should ensure that they do not muddle definitions of 'inter-rater reliability' with other forms of reliability.

- Time sampling and event sampling are NOT sampling techniques but methods of carrying out an observation.

Correlations

A correlation is not strictly speaking a research method but a way of analysing data.

A correlation measures the extent to which two variables co-vary. They are a measure of **RELATIONSHIP**, **TREND** or **ASSOCIATION**.

A correlation can show a **POSITIVE CORRELATION**, **NEGATIVE CORRELATION** or **NO CORRELATION**. The strength of these can be described as weak, moderate or strong.

As with an experiment a correlation will have hypotheses. These are expressed as the correlational hypothesis (alternate) and the null hypothesis and both must be fully operationalised.

The most important thing to remember is that a correlation gives a correlation coefficient which can range from +1 (perfect positive) through zero to −1 (perfect negative) but they do not show cause and effect.

As with the other research methods level of data, descriptive statistics and inferential statistics need to be considered.

Key terms

- **ASSOCIATION** - this refers to whether there is any relationship between two variables.

- **CORRELATION COEFFICIENT** - this is a statistical representation of the degree of relatedness between two variables.

- **NEGATIVE CORRELATION** - this refers to where one variable increases the other variable decreases.

- **NO CORRELATION** - this is when there is no relationship shown between two variables.

- **POSITIVE CORRELATION** - where one variable increases or decreases then the other variable changes in the same direction.

- **RELATIONSHIP** - this refers to the extent of an association between two variables.

- **TREND** - this describes a pattern of variability between two variables.

Confusions to avoid

- If both variables decrease this is still a positive correlation and **NOT** a negative correlation.

- A correlational hypothesis must be written as a relationship and not a difference.

EXAM RESCUE REMEDY

1. The null hypothesis is not the opposite of the alternate hypothesis.

2. Do not confuse an experimental hypothesis with a correlational hypothesis (this could cost you up to four marks in the exam). Or a null hypothesis with an alternate hypothesis.

3. Avoid using colloquial terms which could confuse your definitions e.g. 'randomly selecting anyone who is available' to describe opportunity sampling.

4. Event and time sampling are NOT techniques for selecting samples of participants.

5. Do not confuse types of data with levels of measurement of data.

6. Make sure you are fully conversant with measures of central tendency, measures of dispersion and pictorial representation – the collective term for these is 'descriptive statistics'.

7. Use terminology correctly – see previous example of describing an opportunity sample.

8. Clearly label all tables and graphs.

9. You are expected to be able to think on your feet in the exam and be able to design a workable piece of research. **KISS** your research - **K**eep **I**t **S**hort and **S**imple. Or remember to add **KISSES** to your procedure - Keep It Short, Standardised, Ethical and Simple. As a general rule any research you propose should

be something that you as a student could reasonably carry out with the resources available to you and your level of experience. Also, avoid trying to replicate an established piece of research.

10. Read the questions carefully. And read all of them before you start writing.

The Social Approach to Psychology

The social approach to psychology assumes that as humans are social beings and exist in groups it is this experience that will affect our behaviour. It is concerned with how we relate to the other people within these groups and how being a member of a group shapes the decisions we make.

The results of research in this area can be seen as useful for many professional bodies, such as the emergency services or governments, as they give us an insight into how people will behave in certain situations. As the research is often clearly related to real life experiences we can make predictions based on this.

However, we need to be cautious with how we apply findings from such research. It can be criticised for reducing the importance of the individual and their freedom to make their own decisions by placing an emphasis on situational explanations. To this extent it could be seen as offering an excuse for certain behaviours. In addition to this many people feel that the 'classic' studies are outdated and subject to **HISTORICAL RELATIVITY**.

MILGRAM - OBEDIENCE TO AUTHORITY

Aim

The aim of this study was to investigate how far a participant will go when asked to obey an authority figure even when this contravenes their own moral code.

Sample

The study consisted of a self-selected sample of 40 males aged 20-50 from New Haven obtained through adverts in newspapers and direct mailing.

Method

Although Milgram describes this as a laboratory experiment it is safer to view it as a controlled observation due to the absence of an IV.

Design

This is not applicable as it is not a true experiment.

Apparatus

In one room there is an 'electric chair' to which the 'learner' is strapped. In a separate room is a realistic looking 'shock generator' with 30 switches and lights which increase in 15 volt increments from 15v to 450v. These are accompanied by descriptive terms such as: 'slight shock', 'moderate shock' 'DANGER XXX'

Procedure

The naïve participant is introduced to 'Mr. Wallace', a confederate, and told this is an experiment on the effect of punishment on learning and that the task is for the teacher to teach the learner a series of word pairs. Both the participant and confederate are given a sample shock of 45v and the learner states that he has a mild heart condition. They are told that the shocks may be painful but would cause 'no permanent damage'. They then draw lots to see who will take which role but this is really a rigged ballot as the real participant is always the teacher. The learner is strapped into the 'electric' chair with lubricating gel applied beneath the conductive pads 'to prevent burning'.

The teacher is taken to the adjoining room and sat before the 'shock generator'. He reads a series of word pairs and tests the learner's memory of these. If the learner gets an answer wrong then the teacher delivers a shock. With each successive wrong answer the teacher must deliver a stronger electric shock. If the teacher tries to disobey then the experimenter issues a series of 'prods' which increase in authoritativeness from 'please continue' to 'you have no other choice, you must go on'.

It is important to remember that there were NO actual electric shocks other than the sample shocks and all the learner responses were pre-recorded. The learner is heard to make various protests including banging on the wall (an amazing feat if you recall that he is strapped to a chair!). No further noise is heard after 300v.

The experiment ended when the participant either disobeyed or gave the maximum 450v a total of three times.

Results

There are both qualitative and quantitative results. The first participant disobeyed at 315v, meaning that 40 out of 40 participants gave shocks of 300v. The number who went all the way to 450v was 65% (26/40).

If a participant gives a shock of 390v then he will go all the way to 450v.

The participants showed extreme signs of stress; sweating, shaking, nervous laughter and even having seizures. Also they did question the experimenter and made it known they were not happy with what they were doing.

Conclusions

One conclusion that can be drawn from this study is that people are willing to obey those they believe have legitimate authority. The participants in this study believed in the legitimacy of what they were being asked to do possibly due to the prestige of Yale University and the supposed worthiness of the research they were undertaking. This offers a **SITUATIONAL EXPLANATION** of behaviour.

Evaluation

The participants in this study were deceived on many levels; the learner was not genuine, the purpose of the experiment was false, the shock generator was not real. Although this appeared real to the participants it still lacks **ECOLOGICAL VALIDITY** as you are unlikely to ever be asked to administer electric shocks to a stranger in real life.

Links to approach

What we need to explore here is how the social approach would explain obedience to authority.

The approach is concerned with how other people affect our decision making; this also includes the environment in which we experience things. The participants' in this study found themselves in a highly unusual situation. The experiment took place at Yale University, a prestigious environment which would have influenced the participant's belief about the legitimacy of what they were being asked to do.

Also, they were isolated from other people and had no terms of reference of how to behave in this new situation. Being in the presence of an authentic looking authority figure dressed in a grey lab coat and carrying a clipboard might have added to the participants' belief in the genuine nature of what they were being asked to do. Through a process of socialisation they may have believed this person to be trustworthy and knowledgeable which again would influence their behaviour allowing them to over-ride their moral instinct not to harm other people.

Key terms

- **HISTORICAL RELATIVITY** - we need to consider all the contributing factors for the results gained in research, some of which might include the social and political climate of the time. This kind of research is often a snapshot on life at any moment in time and a generation later people may respond in a very different way.
- **SITUATIONAL EXPLANATION** - this suggests that it is factors in our environment that shape our behaviour rather than our characteristics or personality traits.

Confusions to avoid

- Although Milgram describes his work as an experiment we are only looking at a small fraction of this and the bit we consider does not have an IV. Therefore it might be safer to think of it as a controlled observation.
- This first person refuses to give a shock at 315v not 300v. Text books often muddle this because of how Milgram actually records his data ('shock for which this was the participants last' can hardly be considered clear).

PILIAVIN, RODIN AND PILIAVIN - THE SUBWAY SAMARITAN

Aim

The aim of this study was to investigate, under real life conditions, helping behaviour in bystanders of an unambiguous emergency situation.

Sample

This is an unsolicited opportunity sample of approximately 4450 subway users.

Method

This is a field experiment using participant observation.

Design

This study has an 'assumed' independent measures design. This is 'assumed' because the researchers cannot possibly establish whether a participant has witnessed the event more than once.

IV's	DV's
Victim – drunk/ill	Speed of help
Victim – black/white	Frequency of help
Model – early-critical	Race of helper
– early-adjacent	Sex of helper
– late-critical	Movement from critical area
– late-adjacent	Verbal comments
Size of witnessing group	

Procedure

There were four teams of researchers made up of undergraduate business studies students from Columbia University. Each group consisted of two females who were the observers and two males who took the roles of model and victim.

They boarded the train by different doors and varied the carriage on each trial. There were a total of 103 trials; 38 for the drunk condition and 65 for the ill condition.

The journey between the two stations was uninterrupted for 7½ minutes.

The victim waited 70 seconds before standing and collapsing. He then waited for help from a bystander or the model. The early model stepped in after 70 seconds and the late model waited for 150 seconds before helping.

The victims were always identically dressed except that the ill victim used a black cane and the drunk victim smelt of alcohol.

Results

A selection of the quantitative results is as follows:

- 95% spontaneous help across all trials i.e. no model required.
- 95% spontaneous help for ill victim.
- 50 % spontaneous help for drunk victim.
- 90% first helpers were male.
- Some same race helping notice for black/drunk victim.

Conclusions

Contrary to expectations there was no **DIFFUSION OF RESPONSIBILITY** found.

The study offers the **AROUSAL COST-REWARD MODEL** of helping behaviour.

Evaluation

Because the participant observers were undisclosed this study has high levels of ecological validity.

There are exceptional circumstances in this study insomuch as that the participants cannot ignore the emergency as they are unable to leave the train.

Links to approach

We have to think about how the social approach to psychology would explain helping and non-helping behaviour of bystanders witnessing an emergency situation.

One of the assumptions of this approach is that people are influenced by the groups and environment they are in. These situations will affect not only behaviour but our thought processes and emotions. When we witness an emergency we will become physically aroused which prompts us to take some action to reduce the unpleasant feelings produced by this arousal. We can either reduce this arousal by helping the person in need or by ignoring it by distancing ourselves from it.

Due to the closed environment of the train the bystanders in this situation did not diffuse the responsibility to take action by sharing it amongst those present; rather they felt personally responsible and offered help to the 'victim'.

Additionally this study showed that the condition of the 'victim' also influenced the behaviour of the bystanders. If the victim was unwell (using a cane) he was perceived as blameless for his condition and elicited more help. The 'drunk' victim was seen being to blame for his own welfare and received less help as a result.

Key terms

- **AROUSAL COST REWARD MODEL** - when we witness an emergency this will trigger an emotional, physiological response. We will try to alleviate this unpleasant feeling by taking some action. We can choose to help or ignore the situation and our decision will be based on what the cost will be to ourselves by becoming involved and the reward we might gain if we do.

- **DIFFUSION OF RESPONSIBILITY** - this is the suggestion that the more bystanders that witness an emergency the less likely they are to help. If they were alone then they would feel personally responsible but where others are present this responsibility becomes diluted.

Confusions to avoid

1. Students commonly confuse the role of the victim and the model.

2. When asked to think of practical problems of this research students often state that bystanders may have called the emergency services – failing to acknowledge that there were no mobile phones in 1969!

REICHER AND HASLAM - THE BBC PRISON STUDY

Aim

The aim of this study was to offer an alternative viewpoint to Zimbardo's seminal work on how **TYRANNY** emerges. This study focussed on group identity and inequalities.

Sample

This study consisted of a final sample of 15 males from a much larger self-selected pool of applicants responding to a newspaper advert.

Method

This is an unusual study as the method could be described as a laboratory experiment on one level but as an experimental case study on another. Either way it does use experimental techniques and consists of controlled overt observation.

Design

The study uses a matched pairs design with participants matched on personality variables into groups of three and then one member of each group is randomly assigned to the 'guard' group and the remaining two to the 'prisoner' group.

IV's	DV's
Permeability of roles	Social variables
Legitimacy of roles	Organisational variables
Cognitive alternatives	Clinical variables

Procedure

The guards were briefed in a hotel on the night before the study began. They were then taken to the 'prison' the following morning in a blacked out van where they were given further instructions.

The prisoners arrived one at a time and were given a basic uniform and had their heads shaved. The prisoners were placed in lockable, three bedded cells.

Planned interventions

- **DAY 3** - the promotion of one prisoner to guard.
- **DAY 5** - all participants were told the arbitrariness of their roles.
- **DAY 6** - trade unionist brought in.
- **DAY 8** - study terminated two days early.

Results

The study has a vast range of results and these are a few of the significant ones.

The guards failed to identify with their role; many of the guards expressed discomfort with the inequality their role gave them.

The prisoners developed a stronger sense of shared identity; but only really after the option of promotion had been removed.

Finally there is the dissent of the prisoners and the rise (and fall) of the commune.

Conclusions

This study suggests that contrary to what Zimbardo found, people do not always conform to social stereotypes and groups with power do not always become tyrannical.

Evaluation

This study ticks all the boxes in terms of ethics. It was a tightly controlled study and all the participants were monitored on a daily basis for signs of stress and depression. This was done through self-reports and saliva swabs to test cortisol levels.

Links to approach

We need to establish how the social approach to psychology would explain conformity to stereotypes of social roles.

The social approach considers how social interaction between people in society of differing status will influence behaviour. This study focuses on social interaction and the effect of group identity where there are clear inequalities of resources and status between two groups.

This study demonstrates that the active processes of **SOCIAL IDENTIFICATION** can lead to oppression and that this can form the basis for both tyranny and resistance as the prisoners and guards responded very differently to the situation.

The evidence from this study shows that tyranny will not always result from situations where groups are of unequal power. For **TYRANNY** to occur the individuals would need to identify with the principles that the group holds and engage with them in order to promote them.

Key terms

- **SOCIAL IDENTIFICATION** - this is the process that individuals' belief about themselves is based on their perception of what it means to belong a particular social group.

- **TYRANNY** - this is where one group will abuse the power they have over another group. It commonly occurs in instances of unequal power and resources between the groups.

Confusions to avoid

- Students often muddle the results from the original Zimbardo study with the Reicher and Haslam research. There are some similarities but you must be aware of the differences.

- Students often fail to see the value of this new research. You need to engage with the real life applications that social psychological research has and how this current research reflects changing views in our society.

The Physiological Approach to Psychology

The physiological approach provides us with a biological basis for human behaviour. It will often focus on the chemical basis of human behaviour such as the relationship between serotonin and depression. It also considers whether there is a genetic basis for behaviour.

Research in this area often uses complex technology which requires trained personnel to operate. This tends to produce highly reliable and objective data, making the approach more scientific than other approaches. Recently research has used neuro-imaging techniques allowing doctors to treat brain injured patients in new, innovative ways.

However, many would criticise this approach as being too **REDUCTIONIST** and that it does not consider the person as a whole. Additionally, the findings from such research may not demonstrate cause and effect relationships e.g. whether low serotonin levels are a cause of depression or the effect of experiencing depression.

SPERRY - 'SPLIT BRAIN' PATIENTS

Aim

The aim of this study was to investigate the effect of severing the **CORPUS CALLOSUM**.

Sample

This is an opportunity sample of 11 participants who had already undergone commissurotomy (severing of the corpus callosum) due to severe epilepsy.

Method

Although this study has the tight controls of a laboratory experiment it must be considered quasi experimental as there is not a control group to compare the results with.

Design

This is a repeated measures design as all the participants take part in all the experiments.

Apparatus

Sperry used specifically designed equipment to split the left and right visual fields for the visual tasks and to shield the hands from view for the tactile tasks. This meant that information would only be received by one hemisphere of the brain at a time.

Procedure

Information was presented visually to either the left visual field (LVF) or right visual field (RVF) whilst the participant focused on a central fixation point. The information was presented for only 1/10 of a second meaning that there was no time to move the eyes to transfer the information to the other visual field.

Tactile information was similarly restricted to one hemisphere as an object would be placed into one hand only with both hands shielded from view.

Results

There is a vast array of results, mainly quantitative; this is a small selection of the main points.

Information presented to one VF will only be recognised when presented to the same VF. A significant difference being that information presented to the RFV (and received in the left hemisphere) can be described verbally and in writing. However, if the information is presented to the LVF (and received in the right hemisphere) it will not be recognised, the participant typically saying 'I saw nothing'. Additionally, objects placed in one hand can only be found again by that same hand. Whereas the left hemisphere proved superior for the verbal tasks for pattern recognition tasks involving the hands the right hemisphere was shown to be better than the left when carrying out such tactile tasks.

Conclusions

This study provides much information about the functioning of the brain.

There is clear demonstration of **LATERALISATION** and **LOCALISATION** of **FUNCTION**.

Each hemisphere holds its own memories and has its own stream of consciousness.

Evaluation

There are clearly some problems with this research. As there is not a control group we cannot say how typical the brains of these patients are as they may be different due to the severe epilepsy.

It also appears reductionist as it suggests that the **CORPUS CALLOSUM** is the only way information can be transferred from one hemisphere to the other. However, we know that these participants compensated by adapting their behaviour, for example excessive head movement, moving objects from one hand to another and talking aloud to themselves.

Links to approach

We need to explore whether the physiological approach can explain the difficulties experienced by individuals with a 'split brain'.

These brains work differently to 'normal' brains as the corpus callosum has been severed, thus the two hemispheres of the brain work independently of each other. Unlike a normal brain these two hemispheres cannot transfer information from one side to the other meaning that the people with a split brain are unable to do some things that we take for granted.

Sperry's study demonstrates this. When he presented an object in the patients' LVF (the information being received by the right hemisphere) they were unable to name what they had seen. This is because the language centre is located in the left hemisphere and it could not access the information. A 'normal' person has no such difficulty because the information is automatically shared between the two hemispheres via the corpus callosum.

Key terms

- **CORPUS CALLOSUM** - this is the area of the brain that joins the right hemisphere and the left hemisphere. It consists of a tight bundle of fibres which is like a super highway for the transfer of information.

- **LATERALISATION OF FUNCTION** - this refers to whether certain neural functions are restricted to one hemisphere or the other in the brain.

- **LOCALISATION OF FUNCTION** - this refers to specific areas of the cerebral cortex being responsible for specific behaviours.

Confusions to avoid

- Students often mistake the LVF and RVF to mean that information enters through the left eye or the right eye.

- A common error is to forget that once information has entered through either the RVF or LVF, it then has to be recognised by the opposite hemisphere.

DEMENT AND KLEITMAN - SLEEPING AND DREAMING

Aim

The aim of this study was to provide a scientific investigation of dreaming and give an objective understanding of the relationship between **REM** and dreaming.

Sample

There were nine participants in this study, 7 adult males and 2 adult females. Five of the participants were studied intensively whilst the remaining four were used to confirm the findings.

Method

This is a laboratory experiment.

Design

This is a repeated measures design as all participants take part in all the conditions.

Apparatus

There is some very specialised equipment used in this study which means that trained personnel would need to carry out much of the work. Both

EEG and **EMG** are used to establish stage of sleep and measure rapid eye movement (**REM**).

Procedure

The participants were asked to avoid alcohol and caffeine for 24 hours prior to each experiment. They had to report to the sleep lab one hour before their usual bedtime where they had electrodes attached to their head, face and near their eyes.

The participants were always woken by a doorbell and to ensure there was no experimenter interaction they then had to speak into a tape recorder.

STUDY 1	STUDY 2	STUDY 3
Woken in REM or NREM	Woken 5 or 15 minutes into REM	Woken when one of four patterns of REM established

Results

All the participants experienced cycles of REM and these were distinctly different to NREM.

STUDY 1	STUDY 2	STUDY 3
Most dreams were recalled when woken from REM	Mostly correct at identifying dream length	There was a strong correlation between direction of REM and dream content

Conclusions

It is most likely that dreams only occur during REM and those recalled during NREM are either memories of dreams or **SLEEP THOUGHTS**.

Periods of REM increase in length as sleep progresses.

Evaluation

Both **EEG** and **EMG** are objective measurements. Also as sleep is a physiological function we can assume that it is the same for all humans, so only having a few participants should not be a problem.

However, this study lacks ecological validity firstly because it is unnatural to sleep in a sleep laboratory with electrodes attached to your head. Secondly, asking participants to avoid alcohol and caffeine, which may be part of their usual routine, could alter their natural sleep pattern.

Links to approach

The question we need to ask here is whether the physiological approach can tell us if there is a link between REM and the content of dreams.

As sleep is a physiological function we can expect the experience of sleep to be the same or at least similar for the majority of people. What we know is that sleep occurs in a cycle consisting of four stages. We continually move up and down through this cycle during a normal night's sleep. After the first cycle the first stage shows a period of 'active' sleep, sometimes described as 'paradoxical' sleep, as our brain shows a similar level of activity as when awake. This stage is characterised by rapid eye movement and referred to as REM.

When woken during this stage of REM the participants were able to report that they had been dreaming and could estimate how long they had been dreaming for. In addition it was shown that there was a relationship between the patterns of eye movement and the dream content.

Key terms

- **EEG** - this stands for electroencephalogram. It refers to a method of recording the electrical activity in the brain.

- **EMG** - this stands for electromyogram. It refers to the method of recording the electrical activity in muscles when they flex and contract.

- **SLEEP THOUGHTS** - these are distinctly different from dreams and memories of dreams. They refer to a more ordered type of thinking that takes place in the early stages of sleep which relate to tasks we need to undertake in our waking world.

Confusions to avoid

- Students often inaccurately refer to the electrical activity in the brain as 'brain waves'. This is only correct if describing the pattern seen on a printout from an EEG.

- Do not be tempted to suggest that the direction of the REM causes a certain type of dream as the results here are purely correlational.

MAGUIRE - TAXI DRIVERS' BRAINS

Aim

The aim of this study was to see whether experiences can cause changes to the structure of the brain.

Sample

This was a self-selected sample of 16 right-handed, male, licensed London taxi drivers compared with 50 non-taxi drivers (matched for gender, age and handedness).

Method

This study is a correlation of data from a quasi experiment as the variables are naturally occurring.

Design

Although there is some matching of participants, it is safer to consider this an independent samples design.

IV's	DV's
Taxi driver	VBM (3D)
Non-taxi driver	PIXEL COUNT (2D)

Apparatus

This study used MRI scanners to produce MRI scans and the trained personnel to carry these out.

Procedure

All the participants were screened to ensure they were mentally healthy and did not have any brain abnormality. They were then given an MRI scan.

In Stage 2 the scans from the taxi drivers were compared with scans from a data base of 50 matched males.

Results

The results are all quantitative. The taxi drivers showed increased density of **GREY MATTER** in the right and left posterior **HIPPOCAMPUS**. Additionally there was a positive correlation between length of time as a taxi driver and the volume of grey matter in the posterior hippocampus. However, the controls had relatively greater density of grey matter in their anterior hippocampus.

It is important to note that there was no overall difference in the volume of grey matter in the hippocampus but a redistribution between the anterior and posterior areas.

Conclusions

This study demonstrates that there are regional structural differences of the hippocampus between the taxi drivers and non-taxi drivers.

As the findings show a positive correlation between length of time as a taxi driver and the volume of grey matter in the posterior hippocampus this is suggestive of a **NURTURE** explanation. This suggests plasticity of the structure of the brain in response to environmental demands.

Evaluation

We must remember that a correlation does not infer cause and effect relationships. To establish this we would need to have some evidence that the taxi drivers' brains were not atypical prior to them acquiring 'The Knowledge'.

Links to approach

This approach tries to explain behaviour through an understanding of biological and neurological processes.

This study attempts to show how changes can occur to the structure of the brain dependent on experience or interaction with the environment. It was discovered that taxi drivers who have to constantly use navigational skills to carry out their daily lives showed structural changes to the part of their brain known as the hippocampus, the area responsible for spatial memory. This could be compared with the brains of people who did not have to carry out such specialised tasks and showed no changes in this area.

Key terms

- **GREY MATTER** - this is the term given to the functional part of the brain, mainly because it is grey in colour, which consists of neuronal cell bodies.

- **HIPPOCAMPUS** - this is a seahorse shaped structure which forms part of the limbic system in the forebrain that is responsible for spatial memory.

- **MRI** - this stands for 'magnetic resonance imaging (scan)'. It uses powerful magnets and radio waves to produce a 3D image of the brain or structure of the anatomy.

- **NURTURE** - this forms one side of the nature-nurture debate in psychology. It proposes that the origin of our behaviour is directly related to our experiences and influences from the environment.

- **PIXEL COUNT** - this is a method of analysing the data from an MRI scan which presents the data as a 2D image.

- **PLASTICITY** - this is the suggestion that the brain is able to change structure in response to environmental input.

- **VBM** - this stands for 'voxel-based morphology'. This method of analysing the data from an MRI scan produces a 3D image.

Confusions to avoid

- Although the data are highly suggestive we cannot imply that there is a cause and effect relationship as the data are correlational.

- There is no evidence of a nature explanation here. We cannot suggest that people who are born with a greater density of grey matter in their posterior hippocampi will become taxi drivers.

The Cognitive Approach to Psychology

The cognitive approach focuses on the importance of mental processes in shaping our behaviour; it is important to note that these processes are internal and not external events.

As research in this area is often experimental it is considered to be scientific because it can show cause and effect relationships.

However, due to these studies often being carried out in artificial environments they can lack ecological validity.

In addition, the approach frequently attracts computer analogies which provide logical models of how the mind works. This is unhelpful as it does not reflect qualities that make us human and often our minds do not perform in a logical way.

LOFTUS AND PALMER - EYEWITNESS TESTIMONY

Aim

The aim of this study was to investigate the effect of leading questions on **EYE WITNESS TESTIMONY** (EWT).

Sample

In experiment 1 (EXP 1) there was a sample of 45 students in five uneven groups and in experiment 2 (EXP 2) there were 150 students in three uneven groups.

Method

Both EXP 1 and EXP 2 are laboratory experiments.

Design

Both EXP 1 and EXP 2 use an independent samples design, although it should be noted that there is a repeated element to the second phase of EXP 2.

Procedure

In EXP 1 the participants in all groups were shown seven film clips of traffic accidents in a random order. The accident lasted between 5 and

30 seconds. Following each film clip participants were asked to give a free recall account of what had happened followed by a questionnaire. Within the questionnaire was the critical question asking: 'about how fast were the cars going when they .... each other'. This question was manipulated with five verbs; smashed, collided, bumped, hit and contacted.

Results

The results showed that the more severe sounding the verb the higher the estimate of speed.

Procedure

In EXP 2 the participants were shown one film clip lasting one minute with the duration of the accident being 4 seconds. As with EXP 1 the participants were first asked to give a free recall account of the accident followed by a questionnaire with the critical question 'how fast were the cars going when they .... each other', randomly embedded. On this occasion the verb used in the critical question was manipulated through two variables of 'smashed' and 'hit', with a control group not receiving the critical question.

In the second phase of EXP 2 the participants returned a week later and were asked one further question; 'did you see any broken glass?'

Results

These second results confirmed those of EXP 1 that the more severe the verb the higher the estimate of speed. In addition, if the participant heard the more severe verb they were more likely to claim they had seen broken glass, when in fact there wasn't any.

Conclusions

This study demonstrates that the verb used in the question influenced the participant's response. It clearly showed that the participant's memory had been reconstructed as information merged from the original memory with information learned after the event.

Evaluation

An obvious criticism with this study is the lack of ecological validity; film clips of car accidents in no way mirror the emotional context of witnessing a real car accident.

Links to approach

We need to consider how the approach would explain memory and whether it is reliable.

The cognitive approach is concerned with the process of how we input, store and retrieve information. This study looks specifically at eye witness testimony (EWT) and how memory is not infallible and can be prone to reconstruction.

Loftus and Palmer showed that our memory of an event is comprises the information we take in at the time of the event (input) and how this can be altered by information received after the event (storage). When we then try to recall what has occurred these two memories combine to form a reconstruction of the original event.

Key terms

- **EYE WITNESS TESTIMONY (EWT)** - this refers to the account given to the police of an accident or a crime. It is essential that this is accurate as it can be used in a court to help to convict a criminal or clear a defendant who has been wrongly accused.

Confusions to avoid

- Students often falsely believe that both experiments used the same participants. It is stated that in both experiments the groups are unequal. This does not necessarily refer to the number of participants but could be other factors such as gender or age.

- It would be wrong to suggest that a practical problem with this experiment is that students may not be able to drive meaning that they are inexperienced at judging speed. This is not the focus of the research which is memory of events, making the argument irrelevant.

BARON-COHEN ET AL - AUTISM IN ADULTS

Aim

The aim of this study was to produce an adult test to assess **THEORY OF MIND** (ToM).

Sample

There were three groups of participants in this study which form the independent variable:

- **GROUP 1** - consisted of 16 adults with high functioning autism or Aspergers' syndrome, 13:3 (M:F). These were recruited through adverts in doctors' surgeries, clinics and direct mailing.

- **GROUP 2** - consisted of 50 'normal' age-matched adults drawn from the Cambridge area, but without direct links to the university. 25:25 (M:F).

GROUP 3 - consisted of 10 adults with Tourette's syndrome, 8:2 (M:F), selected as per group 1.

Method

This study uses a quasi experimental method as the IV is naturally occurring.

Design

This study uses an independent measures design, although there is matching on some variables.

Apparatus

Visit http://glennrowe.net/BaronCohen/Faces/EyesTest.aspx to try the eyes test.

Procedure

Each participant carried out two control tasks to ensure there was no cognitive deficit. The first was a gender recognition task where the participants were asked the gender of 25 faces from black and white photographs showing just the eyebrow to mid nose area. The second was a basic emotion task where the participant had to study photographs of the whole face where one of the six basic emotions were displayed; happy, sad, fear, anger, disgust or surprise.

In the 'eyes task' the participants used the same set of photographs from the gender recognition task but this time they had to select the correct emotion which was presented with its foil as an alternative e.g. flirtatious/disinterested.

Finally participants had to complete **HAPPÉ'S STRANGE STORIES** Task; an established ToM test.

Results

All the groups scored identically on the gender recognition task and the basic emotion task showing that there was no cognitive deficit.

The scores on the eyes task and Happé's strange stories task were similar for the Tourette's syndrome group and the 'normal' group but the autism/Asperger's group scored significantly lower.

In addition 'normal' females score better than 'normal' males.

Conclusions

This study shows that the eyes task is a valid ToM test for adults as it has **CONCURRENT VALIDITY** with Happé's strange stories test.

Evaluation

It could be claimed that as the test asks participants to gauge emotions by looking at photographs that this lacks ecological validity because in real life we would consider this in context with other things such as tone of voice and body language.

In addition we know that people with autism and Asperger's syndrome find it difficult to make eye contact with other human beings and as such we are asking them to complete a task which would be unfamiliar to them and perhaps even cause them distress to do so.

Links to approach

Autism is a cognitive disorder that develops through childhood and we need to explore how the approach would explain the difficulties that people with autism experience.

Although parents often recognise problems early in their child's development it is a difficult disorder to diagnose before about 3 years of age. This is because some of the core deficits involve interaction, communication and imagination and do not always come to light until the child is able to speak and is socialising outside of the home environment.

One of the specific deficits considered by this research is theory of mind (ToM), the understanding that other people see things from a different perspective to us and have a different understanding about the world around them. For example Baron-Cohen et al was able to show that adults with autism were significantly less able to cope with the 'eyes task' (an advanced test of adult ToM) compared with 'normal' adults and those with Tourette's syndrome. In this test the autistic adults found it extremely difficult to identify the emotions being expressed in photographs of eyes. This could be why they have difficulty inferring mental states in other people.

Key terms

- **HAPPÉ'S STRANGE STORIES** - this is an established advanced adult ToM test that involves answering questions about mentalistic stories that use techniques such as white lies, figure of speech and irony.

- **THEORY OF MIND (TOM)** - this refers to an individual's belief about how minds in general work and that their own belief may be different to that of others.

Confusions to avoid

- Although interesting that normal males perform worse than normal females on the eye test this does not imply that all males are autistic!

- The Sally Ann test is deliberately not mentioned here, although you will have probably discussed it in your class. It does provide important background information about ToM but frequently students confuse the results of this with those of the eyes test.

SAVAGE-RUMBAUGH ET AL - LANGUAGE ACQUISITION IN CHIMPANZEES

Aim

The aim of this study was to investigate the spontaneous language acquisition in pygmy chimpanzees.

Sample

There were two pygmy chimpanzees used in this study; Kanzi, a male chimp of 2½ years at the start of the study and his younger sister Mulika. The data from these two chimps was compared with that from two common chimpanzees, Sherman and Austin who were about 9 and 10 years old.

Method

Although this study uses non-human subjects it is considered a longitudinal case study as it collects data from a small sample of participants over a 17 month period.

Design

As a case study this is seen as a single subject design with data mainly gained from Kanzi with supporting evidence gathered from Mulika.

Apparatus

There is some very complex equipment used in this study. Within the learning centre there was an array of computerised **LEXIGRAM** boards. These consisted of a grid of geometric shapes that lit up and produced synthesised English words when touched. When each symbol was touched its use was automatically recorded.

When outside the learning centre Kanzi carried simple lexigram boards and a researcher would manually transcribe and enter each symbol that was used.

Procedure

During the 17 month period Kanzi and Mulika were observed in their 55 acre forest and all their utterances recorded. The researchers were always on hand and spoke in English to the chimps whilst using the lexigram boards and also American sign language (ASL).

For a word to be counted as learned it had to occur spontaneously and in context on 9 out of 10 occasions.

An independent researcher blind to the study was taken by Kanzi to various locations in the forest where there were food stations.

Finally there were four formal tests to show whether a symbol had been acquired:

1. Photograph to Lexigram
2. Lexigram to photograph

3. Lexigram to English.

4. Lexigram synthesised English.

Results

After 17 months Kanzi had acquired 46 words and Mulika had learned 37 words. During this time Kanzi had made 2540 non-imitated combinations and 265 prompted utterances.

Kanzi and Mulika made very few errors on the formal tests, whereas Austin and Sherman could only match photographs to spoken English and not complete any of the other tasks.

Conclusions

This study demonstrates that the process of language acquisition in chimpanzees mirrors that of human infants.

This suggests that further research is required but the question would be whether to do so would be ethical.

Evaluation

The animal ethics of this kind of research are a paramount consideration here. However, it is exactly this kind of research that has promoted animal ethics, particularly within the great apes as it shows that they are capable of complex thought processes.

Links to approach

We need to look at how the cognitive approach explains communication and language acquisition.

Communication is not limited to humans and there are many examples in the animal kingdom. However, the focus here is whether animals can learn language and whether this can occur spontaneously.

Savage-Rumbaugh studied four chimpanzees; Kanzi and Mulika, two pygmy chimps, and Austin and Sherman, two common chimps. Kanzi and Mulika were not formally taught symbol use but learned through the observation of their mother Matata who had been taught to use a lexigram. Austin and Sherman were slightly older and had to have formal training in the use of the lexigram.

The study showed that the pygmy chimps had a more refined learning capacity than the common chimps. It was also found that the process of learning language was similar to that of humans and that the pygmy chimps showed the same qualities in their use of language: productivity, displacement, cultural transmission and arbitrariness.

Key terms

- **BLIND (TEST)** - this refers to when an experimenter is used who is naïve to the details of the study and cannot bias the outcome.

- **LEXIGRAM** - this is a board that contains geometric shapes that are arbitrary symbols. Computerised versions light up when touched and produce synthesised speech.

Confusions to avoid

- Kanzi and Mulika did not learn to speak. This would be impossible as chimpanzees do not have the necessary vocal cords for this.

- Kanzi and Mulika were not taken from the wild, although their mother was. They were born in captivity.

What's human speak for "Buzz off and leave us alone?"

Developmental Approach to Psychology

The developmental approach considers the changes in the human condition throughout our lifespan, which allows behaviours to be seen in the context of where and when they arise. It focuses on how behaviours are initiated and then develop and is thus concerned with change over time.

Child development is a popular area as change occurs more rapidly in this group of people. Researchers need to employ a variety of research methods to be able to study this area fully. Additionally it offers useful insights into human behaviour that can be easily applied to everyday life and is useful to many professional bodies, not least education.

However, due to the focus primarily being on child development it means that other areas where development takes place can be overlooked such as adolescence, adults and the elderly.

FREUD - LITTLE HANS

Aim

The aim of this study was to provide an analysis of a phobia in a five year old boy. It was used by Freud to support his theory of psychosexual stages of development.

Sample

'Little Hans', a 5 year old boy who showed a fascination with his 'widdler'(penis).

Method

This study is a longitudinal case study taking place over a two year period.

Design

This is a single participant design and is sometimes referred to as **ACTION RESEARCH** as it is intended as a therapy.

Procedure

Little Hans' father was a follower of Freud and frequently sent him his observations of his son's development. Little Hans is described as a precocious child and his parents were by no means typical of the era as they believed in including Little Hans in everything they did.

Little Hans developed a fascination with his 'widdler' (penis) and his mother threatened to take him to the doctor to have it cut off if he didn't stop playing with it.

At the age of 3 ½ a sister, Hanna, was born and shortly afterwards Little Hans developed a fear of drowning in the bath.

Around the same time Little Hans was chided by his father, and told not to put his fingers near a horse's mouth as the horse might bite them off. He also saw a cart horse collapse in the street and subsequently developed a phobia to horses.

Little Hans was prone to daydreams and fantasies and needed no encouragement to relay these to his father; often telling his father to write them down to send to Freud!

Results

It can be tricky to pinpoint the actual results of this study without drawing conclusions, but try to remember that these refer to what was actually found out.

Little Hans had two primary phobias; fear of drowning in the bath and fear of horses.

Fantasies:

1. **GIRAFFE** - one large and one small crumpled giraffe.

2. **PLUMBER** - a plumber takes away his small bottom and replaces it with a bigger bottom.

3. **PARENTING** - Little Hans becomes the husband to his mother and the father of his own children, whilst his father becomes their grandfather.

Conclusions

Freud concludes that Little Hans shows castration fear (plumber dream) and is experiencing the Oedipus complex (giraffe dream and parenting dream). However, this stage is resolved by the plumber dream (identifying with his father).

The fear of horses represents his fear of his father (castration anxiety), and the horse is symbolic with the whiskers representing the father's moustache and the blinkers his glasses.

Freud confronts Little Hans with his fears and once out in the open they are resolved.

This supports Freud's theory about the psychosexual stages of development and that phobias are a normal, but transient part of children's maturation.

Evaluation

This is a limited sample of one, and Little Hans may be atypical of other children and we cannot make generalisations.

Also, this study may have historical relativity; children 100 years later may mature and develop differently.

Links to approach

What we are interested in here is how the developmental approach explains the development of the personality in young children and whether it can adequately describe how a phobia can form.

Undoubtedly childhood experiences are important in determining who we become as adults. Most psychologists would agree that there is interplay between nature and nurture with neither being solely responsible for our behaviour. Although we have a genetic blueprint which will form a contributing factor we also need to acknowledge the environmental input we experience through the process of maturation.

Freud had already developed his theory of psychosexual development and uses the data collected from Little Hans by his father to confirm this. The fact that Little Hans shows a 'lively interest in his widdler' indicated to Freud that the child is in the phallic stage of development. When Little Hans subsequently develops a fear of horses this is a clear suggestion according to Freud that Little Hans is also experiencing the Oedipus complex (which signifies he is still in the phallic stage). Freud interprets a number of Little Hans' dreams and fantasies which demonstrate how he moves through the phallic stage (giraffe dream and parenting dream) and eventually resolves the Oedipus Complex (plumber dream) thus progressing to the next phase of the psychosexual stages of development.

Key terms

- **ACTION RESEARCH** - this refers to case studies that are intended to act in a therapeutic role to change behaviour in some way.

- **PSYCHOSEXUAL STAGES OF DEVELOPMENT** - this is Freud's theory of how the personality develops through various sexual drives during early childhood. These stages create conflicts that need to be overcome.

- **WIDDLER** - this was Little Hans' name for his penis.

Confusions to avoid

1. Freud did not develop his theory after studying Little Hans. Rather he uses the data he received to confirm his existing ideas.

2. Freud is not suggesting that children have sexual ideas. He uses the term 'sexual drive' to highlight life force, pleasure sources and energy.

SAMUEL AND BRYANT - CONSERVATION

Aim

The aim of this study was to support a previous criticism of Piaget's findings that children can conserve at an earlier age.

Sample

This can be considered an opportunity sample of 252 boys and girls aged 5-8 ½ years from schools and playschools in Crediton, Devon.

Method

This study is a laboratory experiment with 3 conditions.

Design

This study uses an independent samples design for age and condition with a repeated measures design for task.

Apparatus

1. Counters
2. Modelling clay
3. Beakers
4. Water

Procedure

There are three tasks to measure different areas of **CONSERVATION**.

- **NUMBER** - two rows of 6 counters similarly spaced, transformed by altering the spacing on one row.

- **MASS** - two equal sized balls of modelling clay, transformed by rolling one ball into a sausage shape.

- **VOLUME** - two same sized beakers containing an equal amount of water, transformed by pouring the water from one beaker into a taller beaker.

- **CONDITION 1** - standard Piagetian condition. The participants are shown the pre-transformation configuration and asked whether they are the same. They are then shown the transformation and then asked the same question.

- **CONDITION 2** - one-judgment. The participants were shown the pre-transformation configuration and then saw the transformation take place. Only then were they asked whether they were the same.

- **CONDITION 3** - fixed array. The participants only see the post-transformation configuration and are asked whether they are the same.

All the children complete four trials of each task but only in one condition.

Results

All the results are quantitative.

The older children were better able to conserve across all conditions than younger children.

The children in the one-judgment condition were better able to conserve than either of the other two conditions.

Number was easiest to conserve across all conditions and by all ages, followed by mass and then volume.

Conclusions

The ability to conserve improves with age – supports Piaget.

The children fail the traditional two question condition as it confuses them - refutes Piaget.

Conservational skills are maturational and they develop in stages; number, then mass and then volume. This occurs as the child develops **MENTAL REVERSISM**.

Evaluation

This is an improvement on Piaget's methodology as he failed in a fundamental scientific process which is to question whether there were any other reasons for the results he obtained.

Links to approach

Personality is not the only area of child development of interest to psychologists. They also study other dimensions such as biological and cognitive changes that take place, which again tend to be maturational.

Through this maturational process children's cognitive abilities will develop as they learn to cope with the world around them. Their understanding becomes increasingly complex as they build upon their existing knowledge.

The Samuel and Bryant study demonstrates this through the mean number of errors made by all the children in all the tasks. Irrespective of the condition the children were in (standard Piagetian, one-judgment or fixed array) they all made more errors the younger they were. This clearly shows that conservation skills improve with age.

In addition, because of the difference in conservation ability between task (number before mass and then volume) this shows that the cognitive skill of conservation develops gradually.

Key terms

- **CONVERSATION** - this is the understanding that just because we can change the physical shape of something it still has the same number, volume or mass.

- **MENTAL REVERSISM** - before they develop conservation skills the child can only think in the present. They are unable to reverse a process in their mind. So if they see a puddle of water they will not be understand that this could once have been a snowman.

Confusions to avoid

- It would be wrong to think that Samuel and Bryant were alone in their criticism of Piaget's work. This was a development following concerns raised by many other psychologists.

- Children have not become better at conserving since Piaget's original experiment it was simply that he did not question his own results thoroughly.

BANDURA, ROSS AND ROSS - IMITATION OF AGGRESSION

Aim

The aim of this study was to show that learning can occur through the observation of a model and that imitation of that behaviour can take place in the absence of the model.

Sample

This is an opportunity sample of 72 children (36:36 M:F) aged 37-69 months from Stanford University nursery.

Method

This is a laboratory experiment with three experimental conditions; aggressive model, non-aggressive model and no model.

Design

This study is a matched pairs design, the children being matched on their pre-existing levels of aggression measured on a 5-point Likert scale by a nursery worker and the experimenter.

Procedure

The procedure for this study takes place away from the main nursery over three stages.

- **STAGE 1** - all the participants except the control group are taken individually into a room where they are seated at a table and encouraged to play with stickers and potato prints. In the opposite corner there are a variety of aggressive and non-aggressive toys including a 5 foot Bobo doll.

  The participants are then exposed to either an aggressive or non-aggressive model who is either the same sex or opposite sex to themselves. This stage lasted for 10 minutes.

- **STAGE 2** - all the children (including those in the control group) are taken to a second room where they are exposed to mild aggressive arousal. Within the room are some highly desirable toys which the children are allowed to play with, but these are then taken away and the children are told that they are 'special toys' for some other children. This stage lasted for 2 minutes.

- **STAGE 3** - in this final stage the children are taken to a third room, which is arranged identically for each trial with a range of aggressive and non-aggressive toys and a 3 foot Bobo doll. The children are observed in the room by the experimenter and through a **ONE-WAY MIRROR** every 5 seconds. This stage lasted for 20 minutes.

Results

There are a variety of both qualitative and quantitative results in this study.

The children in the aggressive condition showed more imitative and partial imitative aggression than in the non-aggressive and control conditions. The children in the non-aggressive condition showed the lowest level of aggression.

The same sex model was the most influential particularly in the male model aggressive condition. In addition the male children showed higher levels of aggression than females across all conditions.

Many of the children witnessing the female aggressive condition expressed a view that this was not the behaviour they would expect to see from a female.

Conclusions

This study shows that children can learn behaviour through **VICARIOUS** experience and will imitate this. This may be because the models behaviour was not challenged by anyone.

Evaluation

The ethics of this study need to be highlighted as there is no evidence that parental consent was gained.

Also, this was understandably a frightening experience for some of the children being exposed to an adult acting aggressively.

It is also a highly unusual situation for a child to be in; separated from familiar people and left alone with strangers in an unfamiliar environment.

Links to approach

The question we are interested in here is whether the developmental approach can explain how children learn aggressive behaviour.

This study looks at the social processes involved in how children develop aggressive behaviours and whether these can occur in the absence of direct external encouragement.

According to Bandura, Ross and Ross the child experiences the world through a process of social learning as they interact with the environment. An adult is seen as a trusted role model and if they are not admonished for aggressive behaviour then the child will believe it to be acceptable.

Key terms

- **ONE-WAY MIRROR** - this is a mirror that appears as a normal mirror when viewed from one side but can be seen through when viewed from the other i.e. to allow a viewer to see what is happening without being seen themselves.

- **VICARIOUS** - this refers to where learning takes place indirectly through observing someone else and not through your own experience.

Confusions to avoid

- Many students forget Stage 2 of this experiment. This is vitally important as it gives the children a reason to be aggressive.

- The aggressive behaviour is not being reinforced as the children are not being rewarded in any way for their behaviour.

The Individual Differences Approach to Psychology

Whereas the first four approaches consider how we expect all human behaviour to develop and occur in a similar pattern, the Individual Differences Approach to Psychology assumes that the human condition is very diverse and thus we all experience the world in a unique way.

If we celebrate this uniqueness then we also need to consider whether there is any merit in making generalisations about human behaviour.

Typical areas of interest would include gender, personality, cultural diversity and mental illness. This makes the approach very useful as it is applicable to everyday life.

However, one of the main drawbacks is that it can highlight differences rather than celebrating diversity which could lead to stereotyping and discrimination.

ROSENHAN - 'BEING SANE IN INSANE PLACES'

Aim

The aim of this study was to illustrate experimentally the problems with the classification system (**DSM**) in determining normality from abnormality.

Sample

The true sample in this study are the staff, hospitals and to a lesser extent the real patients in 12 different psychiatric facilities in the USA. A common mistake is to identify the pseudo-patients as the participants.

Method

The method used in this study is a field experiment using covert participant observation.

Design

This study is an independent measures design.

Procedure Study 1

There are two procedures to be considered as there are two separate parts to this study.

Eight pseudo-patients who were confederates of the experimenter, telephoned the hospitals asking for an appointment. During the appointment they claimed to be hearing voices, which were the same sex but unfamiliar to them, saying 'empty, hollow and thud'. They were to give honest answers to all other questions except for their name (to protect their anonymity) and their occupation (as most worked in a related field to psychiatry). If admitted they were to behave normally and if asked they were to state that they were no longer troubled by voices. They were instructed to discreetly observe the staff and patients and to record these observations in a notebook. The pseudo-patients would need to gain their own discharge.

Results Study 1

The results to Study 1 are a mixture of qualitative and quantitative.

All the pseudo-patients were admitted and given a diagnosis of schizophrenia except one who was diagnosed with manic depressive psychosis (the previous name for bipolar disorder).

The pseudo-patients spent between 7 and 52 days in hospital, a mean average of 19 days. Not one of the staff challenged them about the authenticity of their status as patients but a third of the real patients did.

Much of the pseudo-patients' normal behaviour was misinterpreted as abnormal e.g. writing in a diary was described as 'patient engages in excessive writing behaviour' and queuing for lunch as 'patient engages in oral acquisitive behaviour'.

The doctors and nurses spent very little time with the patients and any questions asked were mostly ignored. When a pseudo-patient asked when they would likely be considered for discharge they were responded to on 4% of occasions. But this was only a brief response. This was compared to a stranger asking for directions on a university campus where they were responded to 100% of the time.

Pseudo-patients would palm the medication they were given and flush it down the toilet only to find that many of the real patients also did this.

Procedure Study 2

In Study 2 Rosenhan approached a large teaching hospital and presented them with the results from STUDY 1. He told them to expect a number of pseudo-patients over the following three months, but not to challenge them just to record their observations.

Results Study 2

The results of Study 2 are all quantitative.

There were 193 patients admitted during the three month period. Of these 41 were suspected of being a pseudo-patient by at least one member of staff, 26 by two members of staff and 19 by a psychiatrist and at least one other member of staff. In reality there were no pseudo-patients sent to the hospital.

Conclusions

It was demonstrated that it is far more common to make a **TYPE 2 ERROR** and misdiagnose a healthy person as insane. The psychiatrists might argue that on balance this is the safer option.

It is clear that the DSM has poor reliability.

Evaluation

Both the **CULTURAL RELATIVITY** and the historical relativity need to be taken into consideration.

In addition there are some ethical issues such as deception and informed consent.

Links to approach

If we accept that as individuals we are all unique then can we truly say there is an 'average' human being? Thus if there is not an average person how can we decide on what is normal and abnormal?

However, despite assuming that we are all different most societies would be able to identify behaviour which is atypical to their expectations and as such this behaviour would be considered as abnormal. In a western society it is not usual for people to report that they are hearing voices, as Rosenhan's pseudo-patients claimed. As the DSM looks at behaviour which falls outside of normal experience these claims of hearing voices fulfilled the criteria which gave the pseudo-patients a diagnosis of schizophrenia (and in one case manic depressive psychosis). In this case the individual differences displayed by the pseudo-patients gained them a label of abnormality.

Key terms

- **CULTURAL RELATIVITY** - this refers to the view that atypical behaviours in one culture may not be seen as particularly unusual in another.

- **DSM** - this stands for 'Diagnostic and Statistical Manual of Mental Illness'. It contains the criteria used to classify various mental illnesses.

- **TYPE 1 ERROR** - this is a false negative, where a sick person is considered well and refused treatment.

- **TYPE 2 ERROR** - this is a false positive, where a sane person is incorrectly diagnosed as ill.

Confusions to avoid

- Time and time again students incorrectly state that the pseudo-patients are the participants.

- It is important to ensure that you can correctly distinguish between a Type1 and Type 2 error.

A severe case of oral acquisitive behaviour...

THIGPEN AND CLECKLEY - MULTIPLE PERSONALITY DISORDER (MPD)

Aim

The aim of this study was to provide evidence of the existence of **MULTIPLE PERSONALITY DISORDER** (MPD).

Sample

There was one participant, Christine Sizemore, a 25 year old married woman referred to psychiatrists by her GP suffering from severe headaches and blackouts.

Method

This study is a longitudinal case study with over 100 hours of interviews.

Design

This is a single participant design.

Procedure

The psychiatrists carried out over 100 hours of interviews over a 14 month period with Eve White (the pseudonym given to Christine Sizemore). They used hypnosis to recover memories during blackouts.

After a letter was received by the psychiatrists, which was started in one handwriting and finished in another they decided to carry out tests on the two personalities: Eve White (EW) and Eve Black (EB). They used a memory test, an IQ test and inkblot personality tests.

When a third personality, Jane, emerged they also carried out **EEG's** on all three personalities.

Results

Eve Black first came out during a particularly stressful session.

Jane had not been seen before therapy and is considered by critics to be **IATROGENIC**.

- **IQ** - EW=110 EB=104

- **MEMORY** - EW superior to EB

- **PERSONALITY** - EW emotionally repressed, EB tendency to be regressive.

- Both **EW** and **EB** had poor results on digit span recall task.

- **EW** was described as demure, retiring, neat and honest, whereas **EB** was seen to be a party girl, provocative, childish and mischievous.

- **EEG** - Jane and EW=11 cycles per second which is considered normal. EB=12.5 cycles per second. This is slightly fast and similar to those found in psychopaths.

Conclusions

The researchers Thigpen and Cleckley are convinced that this offers clear evidence for the existence of MPD.

Evaluation

Christine Sizemore could be a good actress but this is unlikely considering the length of time spent in interviews, her behaviour being far too consistent.

There are ethical considerations too as the therapists made a decision to integrate the personalities, deciding on which was the most favourable and effectively 'killing' the other ones off.

Links to approach

Schizophrenia is not the only pathological behaviour which we would consider abnormal. Mental disorders range from neuroses such as anxiety disorders and phobias to psychotic disorders which include bipolar disorder and multiple personality disorder.

Quite clearly, having more than one personality is outside of normal experience and as such a person experiencing this would be seen as abnormal. At the time of the study by Thigpen and Cleckley although there had been reports of MPD (known in the USA as Dissociative Identity Disorder or DID) there had not been a clearly detailed study of this condition.

Thigpen and Cleckley have used as many interventions and procedures as available to them at the time to show a clear distinction between the emergent personalities.

Key terms

- **IATROGENIC** - this refers to conditions considered to be created by the therapist. It is often a criticism placed when hypnosis has been used and is cited with cases of recovered memories (as seen with Christine Sizemore).

- **MPD** - this stands for Multiple Personality Disorder. It refers to the fragmentation of the personality into different alters.

Confusions to avoid

- MPD is not the same as schizophrenia, although patients are often given this as a preliminary diagnosis.

- It would be wrong to think that Christine Sizemore was happy with the outcome of the therapy she received. In fact she felt betrayed by Thigpen and Cleckley who sold her story and hold the rights to a film, The Three Faces of Eve, that was made about her.

GRIFFITHS - FRUIT MACHINE GAMBLING

Aim

The aim of this study was to investigate the role of cognitive bias and skill in fruit machine gambling.

Sample

There were 30 self-selected participants of NRG (non-regular gamblers), those who gambled once a month or less (15:15 M:F) and a **SNOWBALL** sample of 30 RG (regular gamblers), those who gamble once a week or more (29:1 M:F).

Method

This study is a quasi field experiment in an amusement arcade with data gathered through overt observation and self-reports.

Design

This study uses an independent measures design with a naturally occurring variable and two conditions: thinking aloud and non-thinking aloud.

Procedure

Each participant was given an initial stake of £3 (equal to 30 gambles) and told to stay on the machine for at least 60 gambles. All the participants used the same machine and those in the 'thinking aloud' condition were asked to verbalise their thoughts, uncensored, into a lapel microphone.

After the 60 gambles the participants could choose either to take any winnings or continue to play.

RG's and NRG's were randomly allocated to the thinking aloud condition or the non-thinking aloud condition.

Results

The RG's had a higher play rate than the NRG's (8:6 per minute) but there was no difference in the playing time between the RG's and NRG's. However, the RG's made significantly more irrational verbalisations in the thinking aloud condition than the NRG's.

The RG's thought gambling was equal chance and skill whereas the NRG's thought it was purely chance.

RG's thinking aloud had a lower win rate than NRG's. 14 RG's broke even compared to 7 NRG's. 10 RG's continued to gamble until they lost everything compared to 2 NRG's.

Conclusions

This study shows that there is little or no skill in fruit machine gambling.

The main difference between RG's and NRG's in relation to skill is probably cognitive.

Evaluation

This study could be criticised as having a lack of control as the arcade remained open to the general public whilst the experiment took place, therefore this may have been a different experience for each gambler.

However, because it took place in a natural gambling environment it is high in ecological validity.

Links to approach

We need to be able to identify whether this approach can show any cognitive differences between regular and non–regular gambling.

Addictions are destructive behaviours which are clearly atypical to normal experience. Not everyone who drinks alcohol becomes an alcoholic and the same is true of gambling. What Griffiths is interested in is whether there are any cognitive differences between the beliefs of the skill set involved with gambling between regular and non-regular gamblers.

Griffiths identified different behaviours displayed by regular gamblers such as personalising the machines they were playing on saying things such as 'this machine likes me'. They would make more irrational vocalisations such as 'I lost because I didn't put the coin in gently enough'. These sorts of behaviours were rarely exhibited by the non-regular gamblers. In addition it was shown that the regular gamblers believed winning was mainly the result of skill whereas the non-regular gamblers saw winning to be mainly the result of luck.

Key terms

- **SNOWBALL** - this is a sampling technique whereby the researcher engages one or more participants and each of these will engage other likeminded participants.

Confusions to avoid

- Griffiths does not use non gamblers. This is for ethical reasons that he cannot expose people to risky behaviour if they have never encountered it before.

- The 'thinking aloud' part is not the abnormal behaviour here. This has been used to establish whether there is a cognitive bias.

Perspectives in Psychology

A perspective is a paradigm, which shows the belief of what psychology is at any one time. As views change then one paradigm will become superseded and another will replace it.

PSYCHODYNAMIC PERSPECTIVE

This is the first perspective in psychology and is dominated by the teachings of Freud. Human behaviour is seen as the result of unconscious processes and these are usually developed during early childhood experience. These unconscious processes are therefore internal events. This means that we form 'models of the mind' and these initial experiences frame how we expect future experience to take place.

Without this perspective psychology would not be what it is today and we have a lot to thank the early psychologists for. An example is the rich tapestry of language in everyday use such 'ego' and 'extravert', which although may be used in a different way than originally intended still focuses on the context of personality.

Much of the psychodynamic perspective remains influential today in shaping many modern interventions such as bereavement counselling and family therapy.

However, it is also considered as very subjective with little scientific foundation. It could also be thought as having historical relativity, which reflects a certain period in time.

The main studies that could be considered to fall into this perspective would be Freud, Thigpen and Cleckley and Dement and Kleitman because they all deal with unconscious processes.

BEHAVIOURIST PERSPECTIVE

Behaviourism superseded the psychodynamic perspective and brought a scientific nature to the study of human behaviour.

This perspective states that only observable behaviour should be studied and would therefore ignore a lot of the psychodynamic perspective. It purports that all behaviour is learned as a direct interaction with the external world. If behaviours are favourably rewarded then they will be repeated and become more common than those that receive negative feedback.

There is a huge objective, scientific basis to support this perspective with much research focussing on the stimulus-response theory. The research has led to the development of successful techniques which have been used to modify undesirable behaviours such as phobic reactions.

However, many people would criticise the perspective for being too simplistic to fully explain the complex wealth of human behaviour. For example it ignores unconscious processes, cognitions and the role of biology.

Some of the studies which could be considered to fall under this perspective might include Bandura, Ross and Ross, Griffiths and Savage-Rumbaugh which all have elements of reinforcement.

Exam Rescue Remedy

1. Make sure you can link the name of the researcher with the title of the research – it prevents confusion.

2. Ensure you know all the relevant details of each piece of research.

3. Do not confuse describing the details of a sample with the sampling technique used.

4. Be aware of the difference between the findings and the conclusions. The findings are the objective results. The conclusions are what we infer about those results usually in relation to the aim of the research.

5. As with G541 this paper is a mark a minute, which should act as a guide for how much to write.

6. Pay attention to the command words in the questions, e.g, identify, describe, outline and evaluate. For 'identify' you can simply state the answer. 'Describe' requires accurate but brief detail. For 'outline' you will usually need to describe and explain. When asked to 'evaluate' you should look to provide a balance of strengths and limitations by making clear psychological points which are supported by examples from the evidence you have been asked to use.

7. If you use psychological terminology make sure you explain what it means to demonstrate your understanding.

8. Make sure you read all the questions in section B and C before you decide which ones to answer. There is little point choosing a question simply because you 'like' the study if you cannot answer all the questions about it. This also helps you to avoid needless repetition because you have made an inaccurate assumption about a question earlier on in the section. For example describing and evaluating when you were only asked to describe.

9. Make sure you read the questions very carefully and plan any answer that is worth more than 6 marks. This will help you structure your response.

10. It is very important to contextualise your answer to ensure it reflects the question and always aim to provide the content asked for.

Glossary of Key Terms

- **DEMAND CHARACTERISTICS** - this is a type of participant bias where the participant picks up cues from the experimental situation that prompts them to alter their behaviour to fit with what they believe is expected of them.

- **DESCRIPTIVE STATISTICS** - these let us describe the data we have obtained and cover three main areas.

    - **MEASURE OF CENTRAL TENDENCY** - selecting the mean, median or mode depending on the level of data you have.

    - **MEASURE OF DISPERSION** - this describes the spread of data using the range, standard deviation or semi-interquartile range, again dependent on the level of data you have.

    - **PICTORIAL (VISUAL) REPRESENTATION** - this shows the data visually as graphs, tables or charts. All of these should have a title, with the axes clearly labelled and use an appropriate scale.

        The types of pictorial representations include:

        SCATTERGRAPH - this is used to plot the two variables of a correlation.

        FREQUENCY TABLE - this shows the number of times something takes place and is the only time when it is acceptable to use raw data.

BAR CHARTS - this records discrete, unrelated data and so the bars do not touch e.g. number of people buying different types of pizza; pepperoni, four cheese, margarita etc.

HISTOGRAM - this is used to record continuous data e.g. time, age etc and so in this case the bars do touch.

- **DESIGN** - this refers to the research design and how you use your participants within an experiment.

    - **REPEATED MEASURES DESIGN** - this is selected to use the same participants in each condition of the experiment and is therefore a related design.

    - **INDEPENDENT MEASURES DESIGN** - in this case different participants are used in each condition of the experiment and this makes it an unrelated design.

    - **MATCHED PAIRS DESIGN** - different, but similar participants are used in each condition of the experiment. They may be matched for various criteria such as age, gender, intelligence or levels of aggression.

    - **SINGLE PARTICIPANT DESIGN** - this is where one participant is studied in detail and it usually takes the form of a longitudinal case study.

DESIGN	STRENGTH	WEAKNESS
Repeated measures	Fewer participants needed	Subject to order effects
	Participant variables kept constant	May need more materials
Independent measures	No order effects	More participants needed
	Same tests can be used	Participant variables exist
Matched pairs	Participant variables more constant	Very time consuming to set up
	Same tests can be used	More participants needed

- **ECOLOGICAL VALIDITY** - this refers to the extent to which the results can be generalised beyond the experimental setting to the real world.

- **ETHICS** - these refer to a set of dilemmas faced by experimenters when carrying out research which require careful consideration to try to resolve prior to undertaking the research.

    - **INFORMED CONSENT** - participants have to be over 16yrs of age in order to give consent to take part in experiments. They need to be given as much information as possible about what is expected of them in order to make an informed choice of whether to take part. Children under 16 may give their assent but consent must be obtained from their parents.

- **DECEPTION** - participants should not be lied to about the nature of the research. However, this is sometimes necessary to ensure that the participant remains naïve to the experiment.

- **WITHDRAWAL** - the participants should be told that they have the right to leave the experiment at any time without prejudice.

- **PROTECTION FROM HARM** - the participants should not be exposed to physical or psychological danger and should always leave an experiment in the same mental state which they entered it.

- **CONFIDENTIALITY** - no identifying information about the participant should be collected or used.

- **INVASION OF PRIVACY** - participants should only be observed in public settings where they can reasonably expect others to see them.

- **DEBRIEFING** - once the experiment has finished the true nature of the research should be explained to participants and they should be given the opportunity to ask questions.

- **HYPOTHESES** - a hypothesis is a testable prediction of outcome dependent on the manipulation of your independent variables. We need an alternate hypothesis and a null hypothesis.

- **ALTERNATE HYPOTHESIS (H_1)** - this can be either experimental (for a test of difference) or correlational (to show a relationship). The alternate hypothesis can either be one-tailed, where it specifies the direction of the difference or relationship, or two-tailed, where it is non-directional.

- **NULL HYPOTHESIS (H_0)** - this is a statement of 'no effect'. This means that the manipulation of your independent variable will have no effect on the measurement of the dependent variable. Or if you are using a correlation then there will be no relationship between your two variables. It is important to note that this is not the opposite of H_1.

- *Whether you are writing an alternate hypothesis or a null hypothesis you must remember that both need to be fully operationalised.*

- **LEVELS OF MEASUREMENT OF DATA** - there are four basis levels of data measurement for quantitative data and these determine what you can do with your data and how it can be expressed.

    - **NOMINAL** - these are data which are simply counted and can be placed into categories. Qualifying for one category will exclude them from any other category. Nominal data shows frequency and is often collected during observations.

    - **ORDINAL** - this level of data refers to data which can be placed in rank order from lowest value to highest value. They simply show the relative position of any score to all the other scores e.g. 1st, 2nd and 3rd place in a race.

    - **INTERVAL** - these are data which have regular,

standardised and equal distances between each value and have an arbitrary zero e.g. IQ, temperature.

- **RATIO** - typically the same rules apply as for interval data, however there needs to be an absolute zero point i.e. no negative values. Examples here might include, mass, volume, distance and time.

- **LONGITUDINAL DESIGN** - this describes the process where the researcher gathers information about the same participants over a long period of time; maybe months or years. This will then show development, or change over time. The advantage of this method is that it removes the bias of participant variables. However, it can create experiment bias if the researcher gets too close to the participants. An additional problem can be participant attrition, where the subjects drop out of the study.

- **MUNDANE REALISM** - this refers to the extent to which an experimental procedure or task relates to everyday life.

- **ORDER EFFECTS** - this relates to a repeated measures design where the order in which participants carry out the conditions might have a systematic effect on the results. This can include fatigue, meaning that the participant is simply more tired when carrying out the second condition and as a result will not perform as well. Also we need to consider boredom, which would mean that the participant becomes bored from carrying out the first condition so they put less effort into the second condition. Finally there may be learning taking place in which case the participant's performance in the second condition will improve as a result of learning from the first condition.

- **QUALITATIVE DATA** - these data are expressed in words, which can be rich in detail. They may tell us why a participant behaves or responds as they do. A disadvantage however is that it can be difficult to compare with other participants, making analysis tricky.

- **QUANTITATIVE DATA** - these are data which are expressed numerically which means they are easy to compare and analyse against other data sets. However the problem here is that they do not show the reasons for the things people say and do.

- **REDUCTIONISM** - this refers to any explanation that attempts to simplify explanations for behaviour or experience which is essentially complex in nature.

- **RELIABILITY** - reliability refers to the consistency of the results, which means that we should be able to replicate research and obtain the same findings.

  - **EXTERNAL RELIABILITY** - this refers to gaining the same results time and again. A researcher can use the test-retest method to establish this, whereby you carry out the research and then at a later date carry out the same research again to ensure you get the same results. Alternatively you can compare the results of one research with the results of similar research.

  - **INTERNAL RELIABILITY** - this considers the structure of the research, for example whether all the questions in a questionnaire are testing the same thing. If you carry out an IQ test then the results from the first half should be consistent with the results from the second half.

- **INTER - RATER (OBSERVER) RELIABILITY** - this questions whether each observer in an observation is rating the behaviour they see in the same way. It compares two or more observers' data to ensure they are similar by working out the correlation coefficient. To ensure high inter-rater reliability the observers need to be trained using coding schemes for the target behaviours.

- **SAMPLE** - this is shorthand for 'sample of participants'. A sample is selected from the target population because it would be impossible to use everyone within any population. The sample needs to be representative of the target population in order to make generalisations about how we would expect the population to behave or respond. There are various methods of obtaining a sample and OCR asks you to be able to recognise the following three.

    - **OPPORTUNITY** - this method uses anyone who is available (and willing) and meets the criteria of the target population.

    - **RANDOM** - this ensures that everyone in the target population has an equal chance of being selected. It is often referred to as the 'drawing names from a hat' technique.

    - **SELF-SELECTED** - people who fulfil the requirements of the target population put themselves forward by volunteering to become participants. This is often seen in response to an advertisement.

- **SNAPSHOT DESIGN** - this describes the process of looking at a cross section of the population (e.g. different ages) at a particular point in time. This is a cheaper and more economical method than a longitudinal study as it will take considerably less time. An advantage of this method is that you gain immediate results. Additionally it is less likely to suffer from subject attrition but there could be a cohort bias whereby the results cannot be generalised beyond the research population. Another criticism is one of historical relativity, as with each generation responses may change due to varying social and political climates.

- **SOCIAL DESIRABILITY BIAS** - this is a type of demand characteristic whereby the participant responds in a way that they believe will portray them in a more favourable light and gain approval from those around them.

- **VALIDITY** - this questions whether the research is testing what it is claiming to test. It is possible that it might be testing something entirely different. For example if we take someone's blood pressure as a measure of stress it could be that blood pressure is raised for other reasons such as exertion, caffeine use or a medical condition. Validity can also be affected by demand characteristics for example when responding to questionnaires participants might lie or exaggerate to make themselves look better creating a social desirability bias.

    - **FACE VALIDITY** - if research 'looks' as if it is testing what it is meant to then it is said to have 'face validity'.

    - **CONCURRENT VALIDITY** - if research gives similar results to other research testing the same thing then it has 'concurrent validity'.

- **VARIABLES** - these exist in both experimental research and correlational analysis.

- **INDEPENDENT VARIABLE (IV)** - this is what the experimenter manipulates to form the two (or more) conditions of an experiment. They can also be naturally occurring such as age or gender. The IV is operationalised by clear categorisation.

- **DEPENDENT VARIABLE (DV)** - this is what the researcher measures to see what difference there is between conditions. The DV is operationalised by stating exactly how a variable will be measured.

- **EXTRANEOUS VARIABLE** - this refers to anything other than the IV that has caused a change to the DV e.g. noise level, time of day.

- **CONFOUNDING VARIABLES** - these are any extraneous variables that are systematically consistent and will confuse your results e.g. using blood pressure as a measure of stress when the participant is taking medication to control blood pressure.

References

In the order that they appear

CORE STUDIES

- **MILGRAM, S**. - (1963) 'Behavioural study of obedience'. Journal of Abnormal and Social Psychology, 67(4), 371-8.

- **PILIAVIN, I**., **RODIN, J.** and **PILIAVIN, J.** - (1969) 'Good Samaritanism: an underground phenomenon?' Journal of Personality and Social Psychology, 13(4), 289-99.

- **REICHER, S.** and **HASLAM, A.** - (2006) 'Rethinking the psychology of tyranny: the BBC prison study' British Journal of Social Psychology, 45, 1-40.

- **SPERRY, R.** - (1968) 'Hemisphere deconnection and unity in conscious awareness', American Psychologist, 23, 723-33.

- **DEMENT, W.** and **KLEITMAN, N.** - (1957) 'The relation of eye movements in sleep to dream activity', Journal of Experimental Psychology 53, 339-46.

- **MAGUIRE, E.** - (2000) 'Navigation-related structural changes in the hippocampi of taxi drivers', Proceedings of the National Academy of Sciences, USA, 97, 4398-403.

- **LOFTUS, E**. and **PALMER, J.** - (1974) 'Reconstruction of automobile destruction: an example of the interaction between language and memory', Journal of Verbal Learning and Verbal Behavior 13, 585-9.

- **BARON-COHEN, S., JOLIFFE, T., MORTIMORE, C.** and **ROBERTSON, M.** - (1997) Another advanced test of theory of mind: evidence from very high functioning adults with autism or Asperger Syndrome', Journal of Child Psychology and Psychiatry, 38, 813-22.

- **SAVAGE-RUMBAUGH, S., MCDONALD, K., SEVICK, R., HOPKINS, W.** and **RUBERT, E.** - (1986) 'Spontaneous symbol acquisition and communicative use by pygmy chimpanzees (Pan paniscus)', Journal of Experimental Psychology, General, 115, 211-35.

- **FREUD, S.** - (1909) 'Analysis of a phobia in a five-year-old boy', In Strachy, J. (ed.) The Standard Edition of the Complete Psychological Works: Two Case Histories, Volume x, London: Hogarth Press, pp. 5-147.

- **SAMUEL, J.** and **BRYANT, P.** - (1983) 'Asking only one question in the conservation experiment', Journal of Child Psychology 22(2), 315-18.

- **BANDURA, A., ROSS, D.** and **ROSS, S.** - (1961) 'Transmission of aggression through imitation of aggressive models', Journal of Abnormal and Social Psychology, 63, 575-82.

- **ROSENHAN, D.** - (1973) 'On being sane in insane places'. Science 179, 250-258.

- **THIGPEN, H.** and **CLECKLY, H.** - (1954) 'A case of multiple personality', Journal of Abnormal and Social Psychology, 49, 135-51.

- **GRIFFITHS, M.** - (1994) 'The role of the cognitive bias and skill in fruit machine gambling', British Journal of Psychology, 85, 351-69.

GENERAL

- **BAINBRIDGE, A., BRADSHAW, P., LATHAM, S.** and **LINTERN, F.** - (2008) OCR Psychology AS. London: Heinemann.

- **BRYNE, S.** and **GROSS, R.** - (2012) Gross Guides to Psychology OCR AS. London: Hodder Education.

- **CARDWELL, M.** - (2010) A-Z Psychology Handbook 4th Edition. London: Philip Allan.

- **DONALD, M.** and **ELLERBY-JONES, L.** - (2011) OCR Research Methods for Psychology AS & A2. London: Hodder Education.

Postscript

Claire Barker has been the Head of Department for psychology for eight years and is experienced at delivering the OCR syllabus. She firmly believes that students should engage in independent learning outside the classroom. She have developed a number of strategies based on sound psychological theory to encourage students to maximise their revision techniques. These have been designed to help all students irrespective of their ability and Claire has worked extensively with EAL students and those with SEN. She has made this revision guide accessible to all AS psychology students following the OCR syllabus.